Irresistible Keto Sweets And Chaffles 2021

Super Tasty Low Carb Ideas To Shed Weight

Kaylee LOPEZ

TABLE OF CONTENTS

Creamy Raspberry Cheesecake Ice Cream

Serves: 8

Preparation time: 10 minutes

Cooking time: 30 minutes **Ingredients:**

- 1 tbsp swerve

- 4 oz raspberries

- 1 tsp vanilla

- ½ cup unsweetened almond milk

- 1 ½ cups heavy cream

- ¾ cup Swerve

- 8 oz cream cheese, softened

Directions:

- In a large bowl, beat together cream cheese and swerve until smooth.
- Add vanilla, almond milk, and heavy cream and mix well.
- Pour ice cream mixture into the ice cream maker and churn according to machine instructions.
- In a small bowl, mash raspberries. Add 1 tbsp swerve in mashed raspberries and mix well.
- Add mash raspberry mixture to the ice cream.
- Serve and enjoy.

Per Serving: Net Carbs: 2.5g; Calories: 188
Total Fat: 18.5g; Saturated Fat: 11.4g Protein:
2.8g; Carbs: 3.5g; Fiber: 1g; Sugar: 0.8g; Fat 89%
/ Protein 6% / Carbs 5%

Perfect Mint Ice Cream

<u>**Serves: 8**</u>

<u>**Preparation time: 10 minutes**</u>

<u>**Cooking time: 45**</u>

<u>**minutes Ingredients:**</u>

- 1 egg yolk

- ¼ tsp peppermint extract

- ½ cup erythritol

- 1 ½ cups heavy whipping cream

Directions:

- Add all ingredients to the bowl and blend until well combined.

- Pour ice cream mixture into the ice cream maker and churn ice cream according to the machine instructions.

- Serve and enjoy.

Per Serving: Net Carbs: 0.7g; Calories: 85; Total Fat: 8.9g; Saturated Fat: 5.4g Protein: 0.8g; Carbs: 0.7g; Fiber: 0g; Sugar: 0.1g; Fat 94% / Protein 3% / Carbs 3%

Peanut Butter Ice Cream

<u>**Serves: 8**</u>

<u>**Preparation time: 10 minutes**</u>

<u>**Cooking time: 45 minutes**</u>

<u>**Ingredients:**</u>

- 2 tbsp unsweetened cocoa powder

- 2 egg yolks

- ½ cup erythritol

- ½ cup peanut butter

- 2 cups heavy whipping cream

Directions:

- In a large bowl, whisk together 2 tablespoons of warm water and cocoa powder.

- Add remaining ingredients to the bowl and blend using blender until well combined.

- Pour ice cream mixture into the ice cream maker and churn ice cream according to the machine instructions.

- Serve and enjoy.

Per Serving: Net Carbs: 3.5g; Calories: 215; Total Fat: 20.5g; Saturated Fat: 9.1g Protein: 5.6g; Carbs: 4.9g; Fiber: 1.4g; Sugar: 1.6g; Fat 84% / Protein 10% / Carbs 6%

Avocado Sorbet

Preparation time: 10 minutes

Cooking time: 10 minutes

Ingredients:

- 2 avocados

- 2 cups unsweetened almond milk

- 2 tbsp fresh lime juice

- 3/4 cup Swerve

- 1/2 tsp sea salt

13

Directions:

- Add all ingredients into the blender and blend until smooth.
- Transfer blended mixture into the container and place in the refrigerator for 10minutes.
- After 5 minutes add sorbet mixture into the ice cream maker and churn according to the machine instructions.
- Transfer into the air-tight container and place in the refrigerator for 1-2 hours.
- Serve chilled and enjoy.

Per Serving: Net Carbs: 2.3g; Calories: 181; Total Fat: 17.1g; Saturated Fat: 3.4g Protein: 1.9g; Carbs: 8.1g; Fiber: 5.8g; Sugar: 0.4g; Fat 86% / Protein 8% / Carbs 6%

Coconut Ice Cream

<u>**Serves: 8**</u>

<u>**Preparation time: 10 minutes**</u>

<u>**Cooking time: 10 minutes**</u>

<u>**Ingredients:**</u>

- 3/4 cup Swerve

- 2 cups unsweetened coconut milk

- 1 1/4 cup unsweetened flaked coconut

- 1/4 tsp coconut extract

- 2 cups heavy cream

- Pinch of salt

Directions:

- Add all ingredients into the blender and blend until smooth.
- Transfer blended mixture into the container and place in the refrigerator for 15 minutes.
- Pour ice cream mixture into the ice cream maker and churn according to the machine instructions.
- Pour in container and store in the refrigerator for 2-3 hours.
- Serve chilled and enjoy

Per Serving: Net Carbs: 3.8g; Calories: 287 Total Fat: 29.6g; Saturated Fat: 23.3g Protein: 2.4g; Carbs: 6.3g; Fiber: 2.5g; Sugar: 2.8g; Fat 92% / Protein 3% / Carbs 5%

Chocolate Mousse

Preparation time: 10 minutes

Cooking time: 10 minutes **Ingredients:**

- ¼ cup heavy whipping cream

- 2 tbsp swerve

- ½ tsp vanilla

- ½ avocado pitted

- ¼ cup unsweetened cocoa powder

- 8 oz cream cheese, softened

Directions:

- In a bowl, beat together cream cheese until smooth and creamy.

- Slowly add cocoa powder and mix well.

- Add avocado and beat until smooth, about 5 minutes.

- Add sweetener and vanilla and beat until smooth for 1-2 minutes.

- Add whipped cream after it is whipped to soft form in chocolate mixture and fold gently.

- Add whipped cream and chocolate mixture in piping bag and pipe in serving cups.

- Serve and enjoy.

Per Serving: Net Carbs: 2.2g; Calories: 146
Total Fat: 14.1g; Saturated Fat: 7.8g Protein: 3g;
Carbs: 3.9g; Fiber: 1.7g; Sugar: 0.2g; Fat 86% /
Protein 8% / Carbs 6%

Classic Citrus Custard

Preparation time: 10 minutes Cooking time: 10 minutes

Ingredients:

- 2 ½ cups heavy whipping cream
- ½ tsp orange extract
- 2 tbsp fresh lime juice
- ¼ cup fresh lemon juice
- ½ cup Swerve

19

- Pinch of salt

Directions:

- Boil heavy whipping cream and sweetener in a saucepan for 5-6 minutes. Stir continuously.
- Remove saucepan from heat and add orange extract, lime juice, lemon juice, and salt and mix well.
- Pour custard mixture into ramekins.
- Place ramekins in refrigerator for 6 hours.
- Serve chilled and enjoy.

Per Serving: Net Carbs: 2.7g; Calories: 265; Total Fat: 27.9g; Saturated Fat: 17.4g Protein: 1.7g; Carbs: 2.8g; Fiber: 0.1g; Sugar: 0.5g; Fat 94% / Protein 2% / Carbs 4%

Pumpkin Custard

<u>Serves: 6</u>

<u>Preparation time: 10 minutes</u> <u>Cooking time: 40 minutes</u> <u>Ingredients:</u>

- 4 egg yolks
- ¾ cup coconut cream
- 1/8 tsp cloves
- 1/8 tsp ginger
- ½ tsp cinnamon

- 1 tsp liquid stevia

  15 oz pumpkin puree<u>Directions:</u>

- Preheat the oven to 350 F/ 180 C.

- In a large bowl, mix together pumpkin puree, cloves, ginger, cinnamon, and swerve.

- Add egg yolks and beat until well combined.

- Add coconut cream and stir well.

- Pour mixture into the six ramekins.

- Bake in preheated oven for 35-40 minutes.

- Allow to cool completely then place in the refrigerator.

- Serve chilled and enjoy.

Per Serving: Net Carbs: 5.2g; Calories: 130; Total Fat: 10.4g; Saturated Fat: 7.5g Protein: 3.3g; Carbs: 8g; Fiber: 2.8g; Sugar: 3.4g; Fat 73% / Protein 11% / Carbs 16%

Quick Mug Brownie

Preparation Time: 5 minutes Cooking Time: 1

minutes

Serve: 1

Ingredients:

- 2 eggs
- 1 tbsp heavy cream
- 1 scoop protein powder
- 1 tbsp erythritol
- ¼ tsp vanilla

Directions:

1. Add all ingredients into the mug and mix well.
2. Place mug in microwave and microwave for 1
   minute.
3. Serve and enjoy.

Nutritional Value (Amount per Serving):

Calories 305

Fat 16 g

Carbohydrates 7 g

Sugar 1.8 g

Protein 33 g

Cholesterol 412 mg

Raspberry Chia Pudding

Total Time: 3 hours 10 minutes

Serves: 2

Ingredients:

- 4 tbsp chia seeds
- 1 cup coconut milk
- 1/2 cup raspberries

Directions:

1. Add raspberry and coconut milk in a blender and blend until smooth.
2. Pour mixture into the Mason jar.
3. Add chia seeds in a jar and stir well.
4. Close jar tightly with lid and shake well.
5. Place in refrigerator for 3 hours.
6. Serve chilled and enjoy.

Nutritional Value (Amount per Serving): Calories 361; Fat 33.4 g; Carbohydrates

13.3 g; Sugar 5.4 g; Protein 6.2 g; Cholesterol 0 mg;

Quick Chocó Brownie

Total Time: 10 minutes Serves: 1

Ingredients:

- 1/4 cup almond milk
- 1 tbsp cocoa powder
- 1 scoop chocolate protein powder
- 1/2 tsp baking powder

Directions:

In a microwave-safe mug blend together baking powder, protein powder, and cocoa.

1. Add almond milk in a mug and stir well.
2. Place mug in microwave and microwave for 30 seconds.
3. Serve and enjoy.

Nutritional Value (Amount per Serving): Calories 207; Fat 15.8 g; Carbohydrates 9.5 g; Sugar 3.1 g; Protein 12.4 g; Cholesterol 20 mg;

Sesame Bars

Serves: 16

Preparation time: 10 minutes Cooking time: 15 minutes

Ingredients:

- 1 1/4 cups sesame seeds

  - 10 drops liquid stevia

  - 1/2 tsp vanilla

  - 1/4 cup unsweetened applesauce

  - 3/4 cup coconut butter

  - Pinch of salt

Directions:

1. Preheat the oven to 350 F/ 180 C.
2. Spray a baking dish with cooking spray and set aside.
3. In a large bowl, add applesauce, coconut butter, vanilla, liquid stevia, and sea salt and stir until well combined.
4. Add sesame seeds and stir to coat.
5. Pour mixture into a prepared baking dish and bake in preheated oven for 10-15 minutes.
6. Remove from oven and set aside to cool completely.
7. Place in refrigerator for 1 hour.
8. Cut into pieces and serve.

Per Serving: Net Carbs: 2.4g; Calories: 136 Total Fat: 12.4g; Saturated Fat: 6.8g

Protein: 2.8g; Carbs: 5.7g; Fiber: 3.3g; Sugar: 1.2g; Fat 83% / Protein 9% / Carbs 8%

Butter Pie

Serves: 8

Preparation time: 15 minutes

Cooking time: 50 minutes

For crust:

- 1 egg
- 1/4 cup butter, melted
- 3 tbsp erythritol
- 1 1/4 cup almond flour

For filling:

- 1 egg
- 1 egg yolk
- 8 oz cream cheese, softened
- 1 cup butter, melted
- 1/2 cup erythritol

Directions:

1. Preheat the oven to 375 F/ 190 C.
2. Spray a 9-inch pie dish with cooking spray and set aside.
3. For the crust: In a large bowl, mix together all crust ingredients until well combined.
4. Transfer crust mixture into the prepared dish. Spread evenly and lightly press down with your fingers.
5. Bake in preheated oven for 7 minutes.

6. Remove from oven and set aside to cool completely.

7. For the filling: In a mixing bowl, add all filling ingredients and mix using an electric mixer until well combined.

8. Pour filling mixture into the crust and bake at 350 F/ 180 C for 35-40 minutes.

9. Remove from oven and set aside to cool completely.

10. Place in refrigerator for 1-2 hours.

11. Slice and serve.

Per Serving: Net Carbs: 2.8g; Calories: 476 Total Fat: 49.1g; Saturated Fat: 25.6g

Protein: 7.9g; Carbs: 4.7g; Fiber: 1.9g; Sugar: 0.8g; Fat 92% / Protein 6% / Carbs 2%

Expert: Crust-less Pumpkin Pie

Serves: 4

Preparation time: 10 minutes Cooking time: 30 minutes

Ingredients:

- 3 eggs
- 1/2 cup cream
- 1/2 cup unsweetened almond milk
- 1/2 cup pumpkin puree
- 1/2 tsp cinnamon
- 1 tsp vanilla
- 1/4 cup Swerve

Directions:

1. Preheat the oven to 350 F/ 180 C.
2. Spray a square baking dish with cooking spray and set aside.
3. In a large bowl, add all ingredients and whisk until smooth.
4. Pour pie mixture into the prepared dish and bake in preheated oven for 30 minutes.
5. Remove from oven and set aside to cool completely.
6. Place into the refrigerator for 1-2 hours.
7. Cut into the pieces and serve.

Per Serving: Net Carbs: 3.2g; Calories: 86; Total Fat: 5.5g; Saturated Fat: 2.1g

Protein: 4.9g; Carbs: 4.4g; Fiber: 1.2g; Sugar: 2g; Fat 60% / Protein 25% / Carbs 15%

Crispy Butter Cookies

Serves: 24

Preparation time: 10 minutes Cooking time: 15 minutes

Ingredients:

- 1 egg, lightly beaten
- 1 tsp vanilla
- 1 tsp baking powder
- 1 stick butter
- ¾ cup Swerve
- 1 ¼ cups almond flour
- Pinch of salt

Directions:

- In a bowl, beat butter and sweetener until creamy.
- In another bowl, mix together almond flour and baking powder.
- Add egg and vanilla in butter mixture and beat until smooth.
- Add dry ingredients to the wet ingredients and mix until well combined.
- Wrap dough in plastic wrap and place in the fridge for 1 hour.
- Preheat the oven 325 F/ 162 C.
- Line baking tray with parchment paper and set aside.

- Make cookies from dough and place on a prepared baking tray.

- Bake for 15 minutes.

- Allow to cool completely then serve.

Per Serving: Net Carbs: 0.8g; Calories: 71 Total Fat: 6.9g; Saturated Fat: 2.7g

Protein: 1.5g; Carbs: 1.4g; Fiber: 0.6g; Sugar: 0.2g; Fat 87% / Protein 8% / Carbs 5%

Expert: Cheese Coconut Cookies

Serves: 15

Preparation time: 10 minutes Cooking time: 18

minutes

Ingredients:

- 1 egg
- 1/2 cup butter, softened
- 3 tbsp cream cheese, softened
- 1/2 cup coconut flour
- 1/2 tsp baking powder
- 1 tsp vanilla
- 1/2 cup erythritol
- Pinch of salt

Directions:

1. In a bowl, whisk together butter, erythritol, and cream cheese.
2. Add egg and vanilla and beat until smooth and creamy.
3. Add coconut flour, salt, and baking powder and beat until well combined.
4. Place mixture into the bowl and cover with parchment paper.
5. Place in refrigerator for 1 hour.
6. Preheat the oven to 350 F/ 180 C.
7. Spray a baking tray with cooking spray.
8. Remove cookie dough from refrigerator.

9. Make cookies from dough and place onto a baking tray.

10. Bake for 15-18 minutes or until lightly golden brown.

11. Remove from oven and set aside to cool completely.

12. Serve and enjoy.

Per Serving: Net Carbs: 0.3g; Calories: 68; Total Fat: 7.2g; Saturated Fat: 4.5g

Protein: 0.7g; Carbs: 0.5g; Fiber: 0.2g; Sugar: 0.1g; Fat 95% / Protein 4% / Carbs 1%

Mixed Berry Yogurt

Serves: 6

Preparation time: 10 minutes Cooking time: 10 minutes

Ingredients:

2 tbsp erythritol

½ lemon juice 1 tsp vanilla

1 cup coconut cream 1 cup mixed berries

Directions:

1. In a bowl, mix together coconut cream, sweetener, lemon juice, and vanilla and place in the refrigerator for 30 minutes.

2. Add berries and frozen coconut cream mixture into the blender and blend until smooth.

3. Transfer blended mixture in container and place in the refrigerator for 1-2 hours.

4. Serve and enjoy.

Per Serving: Net Carbs: 3.5g; Calories: 108; Total Fat: 9.7g; Saturated Fat: 8.5g

Protein: 1.1g; Carbs: 5.2g; Fiber: 1.7g; Sugar: 3.2g; Fat 82% / Protein 5% / Carbs 13%

Coconut Pie

Serves: 8

Preparation time: 10 minutes Cooking time: 20 minutes

Ingredients:

- 2 oz shredded coconut
- 1/4 cup erythritol
  - 1/4 cup coconut oil
  - oz coconut flakes
  - 1 tsp xanthan gum
  - 3/4 cup erythritol
  - 2 cups heavy cream

Directions:

1. Add coconut flakes, erythritol, and coconut oil into the food processor and process for 30-40 seconds.
2. Transfer coconut flakes mixed into the pie pan and spread evenly.
3. Lightly press down the mixture and bake at 350 F/ 180 C for 10 minutes.
4. Heat heavy cream in a saucepan over low heat.
5. Whisk in shredded coconut, powdered erythritol, and xanthan gum. Bring to boil.
6. Remove from heat and set aside to cool for 10 minutes.

7. Pour filling mixture onto the crust and place in the refrigerator for overnight.

8. Slice and serve.

Per Serving: Net Carbs: 2.5g; Calories: 206; Total Fat: 21.4g; Saturated Fat: 15.9g

Protein: 1.1g; Carbs: 3.8g; Fiber: 1.3g; Sugar: 1.7g; Fat 93% / Protein 3% / Carbs 4%

White Chocolate Candy

Serves: 12

Preparation time: 5 minutes Cooking time: 5
minutes

Ingredients:

- 1/2 cup cocoa butter
- 1/2 tsp vanilla
- 1 scoop vanilla protein powder
- 1/4 cup erythritol
- Pinch of salt

Directions:

1. Add cocoa butter in a saucepan and heat over medium-low heat until melted.
2. Remove from heat and add remaining ingredients and stir well to combine.
3. Pour mixture into the silicone candy molds and refrigerate until hardened.
4. Serve and enjoy.

Per Serving: Net Carbs: 0.1g; Calories: 90; Total Fat: 9.3g;
Saturated Fat: 5.3g

Protein: 2.3g; Carbs: 0.1g; Fiber: 0 g; Sugar: 0.1g; Fat 90% /
Protein 10% / Carbs 0%

Mascarpone Cheese Candy

Serves: 10

Preparation time: 5 minutes Cooking time: 5
minutes

Ingredients:

- 1 cup mascarpone cheese, softened
- 1/4 cup pistachios, chopped
- 3 tbsp swerve
- 1/2 tsp vanilla

Directions:

1. In a small bowl, add swerve, vanilla, and mascarpone and mix together until smooth.
2. Place chopped pistachios in a small shallow dish.
3. Make small balls from cheese mixture and roll in chopped pistachios.
4. Refrigerate for 1 hour.
5. Serve and enjoy.

Per Serving: Net Carbs: 1.6g; Calories: 53 Total Fat: 3.9g; Saturated Fat: 2.1 Protein: 3.1g; Carbs: 1.8g; Fiber: 0.2g; Sugar: 0.2g; Fat 66% / Protein 23% / Carbs 11%

Keto Reuben Chaffles

Preparation Time: 15 minutes

Cooking Time: 28 minutes

Servings: 4

<u>Ingredients:</u>

For the chaffles:

- 2 eggs, beaten
- 1 cup finely grated Swiss cheese
- 2 tsp caraway seeds
- 1/8 tsp salt
- ½ tsp baking powder

For the sauce:

- 2 tbsp sugar-free ketchup
- 3 tbsp mayonnaise
- 1 tbsp dill relish
- 1 tsp hot sauce

For the filling:

- 6 oz pastrami
- 2 Swiss cheese slices
- ¼ cup pickled radishes

Directions:

For the chaffles:

1. Preheat the waffle iron.
2. In a medium bowl, mix the eggs, Swiss cheese, caraway seeds, salt, and baking powder.
3. Open the iron and add a quarter of the mixture. Close and cook until crispy, 7 minutes.
4. Transfer the chaffle to a plate and make 3 more chaffles in the same manner.

For the sauce:

1. In another bowl, mix the ketchup, mayonnaise, dill relish, and hot sauce.
2. To assemble:
3. Divide on two chaffles; the sauce, the pastrami, Swiss cheese slices, and pickled radishes.
4. Cover with the other chaffles, divide the sandwich in halves and serve.

Nutrition:

Calories 316

Fats 21.78g

Carbs 6.52g

Net Carbs 5.42g

Protein 23.56g

Pumpkin-Cinnamon Churro Sticks

Preparation Time: 10 minutes

Cooking Time: 14 minutes

Servings: 2

Ingredients:

- 3 tbsp coconut flour

- ¼ cup pumpkin puree

- 1 egg, beaten

- ½ cup finely grated mozzarella cheese

- 2 tbsp sugar-free maple syrup + more for serving

- 1 tsp baking powder

- 1 tsp vanilla extract

- ½ tsp pumpkin spice seasoning

- 1/8 tsp salt

- 1 tbsp cinnamon powder

Directions:

1. Preheat the waffle iron.
2. Mix all the ingredients in a medium bowl until well combined.
3. Open the iron and add half of the mixture. Close and cook until golden brown and crispy, 7 minutes.
4. Remove the chaffle onto a plate and make 1 more with the remaining batter.
5. Cut each chaffle into sticks, drizzle the top with more maple syrup and serve after.

<u>Nutrition Facts per Serving:</u>

Calories 219

Fats 9.72g

Carbs 8.64g

Net Carbs 4.34g

Protein 25.27g

Keto Chocolate Fudge Chaffle

Preparation Time: 10 minutes

Cooking Time: 14 minutes

Servings: 2

Ingredients:

- 1 egg, beaten
- ¼ cup finely grated Gruyere cheese
- 2 tbsp unsweetened cocoa powder
- ¼ tsp baking powder
- ¼ tsp vanilla extract
- 2 tbsp erythritol
- 1 tsp almond flour
- 1 tsp heavy whipping cream
- A pinch of salt

Directions:

1. Preheat the waffle iron.
2. Add all the ingredients to a medium bowl and mix well.
3. Open the iron and add half of the mixture. Close and cook until golden brown and crispy, 7 minutes.
4. Remove the chaffle onto a plate and make another with the remaining batter.
5. Cut each chaffle into wedges and serve after.

<u>Nutrition Facts per Serving:</u>

Calories 173

Fats 13.08g

Carbs 3.98g

Net Carbs 2.28g

Protein 12.27g

Guacamole Chaffle Bites

Preparation Time: 10 minutes

Cooking Time: 14 minutes

Servings: 2

Ingredients:

- 1 large turnip, cooked and mashed
- 2 bacon slices, cooked and finely chopped
- ½ cup finely grated Monterey Jack cheese
- 1 egg, beaten
- 1 cup guacamole for topping

Directions:

1. Preheat the waffle iron.
2. Mix all the ingredients except for the guacamole in a medium bowl.
3. Open the iron and add half of the mixture. Close and cook for 4 minutes. Open the lid, flip the chaffle and cook further until golden brown and crispy, 3 minutes.
4. Remove the chaffle onto a plate and make another in the same manner.
5. Cut each chaffle into wedges, top with the guacamole and serve afterward.

<u>Nutrition Facts per Serving:</u>

Calories 311

Fats 22.52g

Carbs 8.29g

Net Carbs 5.79g

Protein 13.62g

Zucchini Parmesan Chaffles

Preparation Time: 10 minutes

Cooking Time: 14 minutes

Servings: 2

Ingredients:

- 1 cup shredded zucchini
- 1 egg, beaten
- ½ cup finely grated Parmesan cheese
- Salt and freshly ground black pepper to taste

Directions:

1. Preheat the waffle iron.
2. Put all the ingredients in a medium bowl and mix well.
3. Open the iron and add half of the mixture. Close and cook until crispy, 7 minutes.
4. Remove the chaffle onto a plate and make another with the remaining mixture.
5. Cut each chaffle into wedges and serve afterward.

Nutrition Facts per Serving:

Calories 138

Fats 9.07g

Carbs 3.81g

Net Carbs 3.71g

Protein 10.02g

40. Blue Cheese Chaffle Bites

Preparation Time: 10 minutes

Cooking Time: 14 minutes

Servings: 2

Ingredients:

- 1 egg, beaten
- ½ cup finely grated Parmesan cheese
- ¼ cup crumbled blue cheese
- 1 tsp erythritol

Directions:

1. Preheat the waffle iron.
2. Mix all the ingredients in a bowl.
3. Open the iron and add half of the mixture. Close and cook until crispy, 7 minutes.
4. Remove the chaffle onto a plate and make another with the remaining mixture.
5. Cut each chaffle into wedges and serve afterward.

Nutrition Facts per Serving:

Calories 196

Fats 13.91g

Carbs 4.03g

Net Carbs 4.03g

Protein 13.48g

Pumpkin Chaffle with Frosting

Preparation Time: 15 minutes

Servings: 2

Ingredients:

- 1 egg, lightly beaten
- 1 tbsp sugar-free pumpkin puree
- 1/4 tsp pumpkin pie spice
- 1/2 cup mozzarella cheese, shredded

For frosting:

- 1/2 tsp vanilla
- 2 tbsp Swerve
- 2 tbsp cream cheese, softened

Directions:

1. Preheat your waffle maker.
2. Add egg in a bowl and whisk well.
3. Add pumpkin puree, pumpkin pie spice, and cheese and stir well.
4. Spray waffle maker with cooking spray.
5. Pour 1/2 of the batter in the hot waffle maker and cook for 3-4 minutes or until golden brown. Repeat with the remaining batter.
6. In a small bowl, mix all frosting ingredients until smooth.
7. Add frosting on top of hot chaffles and serve.

Nutrition:

Calories 98

Fat 7 g

Carbohydrates 3.6 g

Sugar 0.6 g

Protein 5.6 g

Cholesterol 97 mg

Breakfast Peanut Butter Chaffle

Preparation Time: 15 minutes

Servings: 2

Ingredients:

- 1 egg, lightly beaten
- ½ tsp vanilla
- 1 tbsp Swerve
- 2 tbsp powdered peanut butter
- ½ cup mozzarella cheese, shredded

Directions:

1. Preheat your waffle maker.
2. Add all ingredients into the bowl and mix until well combined.
3. Spray waffle maker with cooking spray.
4. Pour half batter in the hot waffle maker and cook for 5-7 minutes or until golden brown. Repeat with the remaining batter.
5. Serve and enjoy.

Nutrition:

Calories 80

Fat 4.1 g

Carbohydrates 2.9 g

Sugar 0.6 g

Protein 7.4 g

Cholesterol 86 mg

Chaffles with Caramelized Apples and Yogurt

Serving: 2

Preparation Time: 5 minutes

Cooking Time: 10 minutes

Ingredients

- 1 tablespoon unsalted butter
- 1 tablespoon golden brown sugar
- 1 Granny Smith apple, cored and thinly sliced
- 1 pinch salt
- 2 whole-grain frozen waffles, toasted
- 1/2 cup mozzarella cheese, shredded
- 1/4 cup Yoplait® Original French Vanilla yogurt

Direction

1. Melt the butter in a large skillet over medium-high heat until starting to brown. Add mozzarella cheese and stir well.

2. Add the sugar, apple slices and salt and cook, stirring frequently, until apples are softened and tender, about 6 to 9 minutes.

3. Put one warm waffle each on a plate, top each with yogurt and apples. Serve warm.

Nutrition:

Calories: 240 calories

Total Fat: 10.4 g

Cholesterol: 54 mg

Sodium: 226 mg

Total Carbohydrate: 33.8 g

Protein: 4.7 g

Chaffle Ice Cream Bowl

Preparation Time: 5 minutes

Cooking Time: 0 minutes

Servings: 2

Ingredients:

- 4 basic chaffles
- 2 scoops keto ice cream
- 2 teaspoons sugar-free chocolate syrup

Method:

1. Arrange 2 basic chaffles in a bowl, following the contoured design of the bowl.
2. Top with the ice cream.
3. Drizzle with the syrup on top.
4. Serve.

Nutritional Value:

- Calories 181
- Total Fat 17.2g
- Saturated Fat 4.2g
- Cholesterol 26mg
- Sodium 38mg
- Total Carbohydrate 7g
- Dietary Fiber 1g
- Total Sugars 4.1g
- Protein 0.4g
- Potassium 0mg

Zucchini Chaffle

Preparation Time: 10 minutes

Cooking Time: 8 minutes

Servings: 2

Ingredients:

- 1 cup zucchini, grated
- ¼ cup mozzarella cheese, shredded
- 1 egg, beaten
- ½ cup Parmesan cheese, shredded
- 1 teaspoon dried basil
- Salt and pepper to taste

Method:

1. Preheat your waffle maker.
2. Sprinkle pinch of salt over the zucchini and mix.
3. Let sit for 2 minutes.
4. Wrap zucchini with paper towel and squeeze to get rid of water.
5. Transfer to a bowl and stir in the rest of the ingredients.
6. Pour half of the mixture into the waffle maker.
7. Close the device.
8. Cook for 4 minutes.
9. Make the second chaffle following the same steps.

Nutritional Value:

- Calories 194
- Total Fat 13 g
- Saturated Fat 7 g
- Cholesterol 115 mg
- Sodium 789 mg
- Potassium 223 mg
- Total Carbohydrate 4 g
- Dietary Fiber 1 g
- Protein 16 g
- Total Sugars 2 g

Chaffle Cream Cake

Preparation Time: 20 minutes

Cooking Time: 30 minutes

Servings: 8

Ingredients:
Chaffle

- 4 oz. cream cheese
- 4 eggs
- 1 tablespoon butter, melted
- 1 teaspoon vanilla extract
- ½ teaspoon cinnamon
- 1 tablespoon sweetener
- 4 tablespoons coconut flour
- 1 tablespoon almond flour
- 1 ½ teaspoons baking powder
- 1 tablespoon coconut flakes (sugar-free)
- 1 tablespoon walnuts, chopped

Frosting

- 2 oz. cream cheese
- 2 tablespoons butter
- 2 tablespoons sweetener
- ½ teaspoon vanilla

Method:

1. Combine all the chaffle ingredients except coconut flakes and walnuts in a blender.
2. Blend until smooth.
3. Plug in your waffle maker.
4. Add some of the mixture to the waffle maker.
5. Cook for 3 minutes.
6. Repeat steps until the remaining batter is used.
7. While letting the chaffles cool, make the frosting by combining all the ingredients.
8. Use a mixer to combine and turn frosting into fluffy consistency.
9. Spread the frosting on top of the chaffles.

Nutritional Value:

- Calories127
- Total Fat 13.7g
- Saturated Fat 9 g
- Cholesterol 102.9mg
- Sodium 107.3mg
- Potassium 457 mg
- Total Carbohydrate 5.5g
- Dietary Fiber 1.3g
- Protein 5.3g
- Total Sugars 1.5g

Taco Chaffle

Preparation Time: 15 minutes

Cooking Time: 20 minutes

Servings: 4

Ingredients:

- 1 tablespoon olive oil
- 1 lb. ground beef
- 1 teaspoon ground cumin
- 1 teaspoon chili powder
- ¼ teaspoon onion powder
- ½ teaspoon garlic powder
- Salt to taste
- 4 basic chaffles
- 1 cup cabbage, chopped
- 4 tablespoons salsa (sugar-free)

Method:

1. Pour the olive oil into a pan over medium heat.

2. Add the ground beef.

3. Season with the salt and spices.

4. Cook until brown and crumbly.

5. Fold the chaffle to create a "taco shell".

6. Stuff each chaffle taco with cabbage.

7. Top with the ground beef and salsa.

Nutritional Value:

- Calories 255

- Total Fat 10.9g

- Saturated Fat 3.2g

- Cholesterol 101mg

- Sodium 220mg

- Potassium 561mg

- Total Carbohydrate 3g

- Dietary Fiber 1g

- Protein 35.1g

- Total Sugars 1.3g

Vanilla Cream Cheese Mousse

Preparation time: 10 minutes Cooking time: 0

minutes Servings: 2

INGREDIENTS

- 1 teaspoon vanilla extract
- 1 cup coconut cream
- 2 ounces cream cheese
- 1 tablespoon ghee, melted
- 1 tablespoon stevia

DIRECTIONS

1. In your blender, mix the cream with the cream cheese and the other Ingredients, pulse well, divide into cups and serve cold.

NUTRITION: calories 254, fat 24, fiber 1, carbs 2, protein 8

Espresso Mousse

Preparation time: 10 minutes Cooking time: 0

minutes Servings: 4

INGREDIENTS

- ½ cup almond milk
- ½ cup coconut cream
- 1 teaspoon vanilla extract
- 1 teaspoon espresso powder
- 1 teaspoon stevia
- 1 teaspoon lime zest, grated

DIRECTIONS

1. In a blender, combine the cream with the milk, espresso and the
   other Ingredients, pulse well, divide into cups and serve.

NUTRITION: calories 160, fat 13, fiber 0, carbs 2,

protein 7

Almond Mousse

Preparation time: 2 hours Cooking time: 0
minutes Servings: 2

INGREDIENTS

- 1 cup almonds, chopped
- 1 cup coconut cream
- 1 teaspoon cinnamon powder
- 1 tablespoon stevia
- 4 tablespoons almond milk

DIRECTIONS

1. In a blender, mix the almonds with the cream and the other
   Ingredients, pulse well, divide into bowls and keep in the fridge for
   2 hours before serving.

NUTRITION: calories 200, fat 2, fiber 2, carbs 5,
protein 5

Cherry Mousse

Preparation time: 10 minutes Cooking time: minutes

Servings: 2

INGREDIENTS

- 1 cup cherries, pitted
- ½ teaspoon vanilla extract
- 1 cup coconut cream
- 1 tablespoon lemon juice
- ½ tablespoon stevia

DIRECTIONS

1. In a blender, combine the cherries with the cream and the other Ingredients, pulse well, divide into bows and serve.

NUTRITION: Calories 60, Fat 1, Fiber 1, Carbs 2, Protein 0.5

Lemon Walnuts and Cream Cheese Mousse

Preparation time: 10 minutes Cooking time: 0 minutes Servings: 2

INGREDIENTS

- 1 teaspoon almond extract
- Juice of ½ lemon
- 1 cup coconut cream
- ½ cup walnuts, chopped
- 1 cup cream cheese
- ½ tablespoon stevia

DIRECTIONS

1. In a blender, combine the cream with the walnuts, lemon juice and the other Ingredients, pulse well and divide into bowls.
2. Serve the mousse cold.

NUTRITION: calories 234, fat 23, fiber 2, carbs 6, protein 7

Walnuts and Chia Mousse

Preparation time: 2 hours Cooking time: 0
minutes Servings: 4

INGREDIENTS

- 1 teaspoon vanilla extract
- 2 tablespoons ghee, melted
- 1 cup walnuts, chopped
- 2 tablespoons chia seeds
- 1 cup almond milk
- ½ cup heavy cream
- 2 teaspoons granulated stevia

DIRECTIONS

1.   In a blender, mix the walnuts with the chia seeds, vanilla and
the other ingredients , pulse well, divide into bowls and keep in the
fridge for 2 hours before serving.

NUTRITION: calories 450, fat 43, fiber 3, carbs 7,
protein 7

Dates and Almond Mousse

Preparation time: 3 hours Cooking time: 0
minutes Servings: 4

INGREDIENTS

- 1 cup almonds, blanched
- 1 cup coconut cream
- ½ cup dates, chopped
- 1 cup coconut milk
- 1 tablespoon swerve
- ½ teaspoon vanilla extract

DIRECTIONS

1. In a blender, combine the almond with the cream, dates and the
   other Ingredients, pulse well, divide into small bowls and keep
   in the fridge for 3 hours before serving.

NUTRITION: calories 555, fat 52.4, fiber 8.9,
carbs 17.4, protein 3

Dates Mousse

Preparation time: 30 minutes Cooking time: 0
minutes Servings: 4

INGREDIENTS

- 2 cups heavy cream
- ¼ cup stevia
- 2 cups dates, chopped
- 1 tablespoon cinnamon powder
- 1 teaspoon vanilla extract

DIRECTIONS

1. In a blender, combine the cream with the dates, stevia and the
   other Ingredients,

   whisk, divide into cups and keep in the fridge for 30 minutes
   before serving.

NUTRITION: calories 141, fat 4.7, fiber 4.7, carbs
8.3, protein 0.8

Dates and Berries Mousse

Preparation time: 10 minutes Cooking time: 0

minutes Servings: 2

INGREDIENTS

- 1 teaspoon vanilla extract
- 1 teaspoon almond extract
- 1 cup dates, chopped
- 1 cup blueberries
- 1 cup coconut cream
- 1 tablespoon stevia

DIRECTIONS

1. In a blender, mix the dates with the berries, cream and the other Ingredients, pulse well, divide into bowls and keep in the fridge for 10 minutes before serving.

NUTRITION: calories 200, fat 8, fiber 3.4, carbs 7.6, protein 4.3

Classic Coconut Truffles

Preparation Time: 15 minutes + chilling time Servings 16

NUTRITION: 90 Calories; 6.3g Fat; 4.9g Carbs; 3.7g Protein; 0.5g Fiber

INGREDIENTS

- 4 tablespoons coconut flakes
- 1/4 cup unsweetened cocoa powder
- 1/4 cup coconut oil
- 1 cup whipped cream
- 1 ½ cups bakers' chocolate, unsweetened
- 3 tablespoons Swerve
- 1 teaspoon vanilla extract
- 1 tablespoon rum

DIRECTIONS

1. Melt the chocolate in your microwave. Add in the coconut flakes, coconut oil, cream, Swerve, vanilla extract, and rum.
2. Place in your refrigerator until the batter is well-chilled. Roll the mixture into balls and cover with cocoa powder on all sides.
3. Storing
4. Place the coconut truffles in airtight containers or Ziploc bags; keep in your refrigerator for 3 weeks to 1 month.

5. To freeze, arrange the coconut truffles on a baking tray in a single layer; freeze for about 2 hours. Transfer the frozen coconut truffles to an airtight container. Freeze for up to a month. Bon appétit!

Greek-Style Coconut Cheesecake

Preparation Time: 30 minutes Servings 12

NUTRITION: 246 Calories; 22.2g Fat; 5.7g Carbs; 8.1g Protein; 1.9g Fiber

INGREDIENTS

- 5 ounces Greek-style yogurt
- 1 ounce coconut flakes
- 10 ounces almond meal
- 1/4 teaspoon grated nutmeg
- 1 teaspoon lemon zest
- 5 ounces soft cheese
- 1 teaspoon baking powder
- 4 eggs, lightly beaten
- 4 ounces Swerve
- 1/4 coconut oil

DIRECTIONS

1. Brush two spring form pans with a nonstick spray.

2. Mix the almond meal, coconut flakes, nutmeg, and baking powder. Add in the eggs, one at a time, whisking constantly; add in 2 ounces of Swerve.

3. Spoon the mixture into spring form pans and bake at 360 degrees F for 23 minutes.

4. In another bowl, combine the coconut oil, lemon zest, yogurt, soft cheese, and the remaining 2 ounces of Swerve. Mix to combine and spoon the filling over the first crust. Spread half of the filling over it.

5. Top with another crust and spread the rest of the filling over the top.

6. Storing

7. Place your cheesecake in airtight containers and refrigerate for a week.

8. To freeze, place your cheesecake on a baking tray and freeze for 2 hours. Now, place them in airtight containers. They can be frozen for 2 to 3 months. Bon appétit!

Butterscotch Cheesecake Cupcakes

Preparation Time: 30 minutes + chilling time Servings 8
NUTRITION: 165 Calories; 15.6g Fat; 5.4g Carbs; 5.2g Protein; 1.7g Fiber

INGREDIENTS

- 2 eggs
- 1 tablespoon whiskey
- 2 packets stevia
- 3 tablespoons butter, melted
- 10 ounces soft cheese, at room temperature
- 1/2 teaspoon ground cinnamon
- For the Frosting:
- 1 teaspoon butterscotch extract
- 1/2 stick butter, at room temperature
- 1/2 cup powdered erythritol
- 1 ½ tablespoons coconut milk, unsweetened

DIRECTIONS

1. Start by preheating your oven to 365 degrees f.

2. Mix 3 tablespoons of butter, soft cheese, whiskey, eggs, stevia, and cinnamon until well combined.

3. Scrape the batter into the muffin pan and bake approximately 15 minutes; place the muffin pan in the freezer for 2 hours.

4. In a mixing bowl, beat 1/2 stick of butter with powdered erythritol and butterscotch extract.

5. Gradually pour in the milk and mix again. Afterwards, frost the chilled cupcakes.

6. Storing

7. Place your cupcakes in airtight containers and refrigerate for a week.

8. To freeze, place your cupcakes on a baking tray and freeze for 2 hours. Now, place them in airtight containers. They can be frozen for 2 to 3 months. Bon appétit!

The Best Keto Birthday Cake

Preparation Time: 40 minutes + chilling time Servings 10

NUTRITION: 241 Calories; 22.6g Fat; 4.2g Carbs; 6.6g Protein; 0.7g Fiber

INGREDIENTS

- For the Cake Base:
- 2/3 cup coconut flour
- 2 ½ tablespoons butter
- 4 eggs
- 1 cup full-fat milk
- 1 teaspoon vanilla extract
- 1 ½ cups almond meal
- 1/2 teaspoon baking powder
- A pinch of coarse salt
- 1 cup erythritol
- For the Frosting:
- 1/3 cup erythritol
- 3 ounces   coconut oil, at room temperature
- A few drops coconut flavor
- 10 ounces soft cheese

DIRECTIONS

1. Mix all Ingredients for the cake base until well combined.

2. Press the crust into a parchment-lined springform pan. Bake at 365 degrees F for 30 minutes or until a toothpick comes out

    clean; allow it to cool to room temperature.

3. Meanwhile, beat the cheese using your electric mixer until creamy. Stir in the remaining Ingredients and continue to mix until well combined.

4. Frost your cake and serve well-chilled.

5. Storing

6. Place your cheesecake in airtight containers and refrigerate for a week.

7. To freeze, place your cheesecake on a baking tray and freeze for 2 hours. Now, place them in airtight containers. They can be frozen for 2 to 3 months. Bon appétit!

Tangerine Chocolate Pudding

Preparation Time: 15 minutes + chilling time Servings 6

NUTRITION: 158 Calories; 15.7g Fat; 7.2g Carbs; 2.2g Protein; 1.6g Fiber

INGREDIENTS

- 3 1/3 tablespoons Dutch-processed brown cocoa powder
- 2 cups whipped cream
- Fresh juice and zest of 1/2 tangerine
- 1/4 teaspoon ground cloves
- 1/2 teaspoon crystallized ginger
- 6 ounces chocolate, unsweetened
- 3 tablespoons powdered erythritol

DIRECTIONS

1. Using a stand mixer with a whisk attachment, whip the cream until soft peaks form.
2. Add in the powdered erythritol and cocoa powder and beat again. Add in the remaining Ingredients and beat until everything is well incorporated.
3. Storing
4. Spoon your pudding into six airtight containers; keep in your refrigerator for 5 to 6 days.

5. To freeze, place your pudding in six airtight containers; freeze up to 1 month.

Peanut Butter Mousse

Preparation Time: 15 minutes Servings 4

NUTRITION: 288 Calories; 27.3g Fat; 6.9g Carbs; 6.2g Protein; 5.2g Fiber

INGREDIENTS

- 1/2 cup peanut butter
- 1 ½ cups avocado, peeled, pitted, and diced
- 1 teaspoon vanilla extract
- 1 tablespoon lemon juice
- 1/2 cup coconut cream
- 1 teaspoon monk fruit powder
- 1/2 cup coconut milk

DIRECTIONS

1. Place all Ingredients in your blender or food processor. Process until well combined.
2. Storing
3. Spoon your mousse into four airtight containers; keep in your refrigerator for 5 to 6 days.

Decadent Macchiato Penuche

Preparation Time: 10 minutes + chilling time Servings 8

NUTRITION: 145 Calories; 12.8g Fat; 6.2g Carbs; 0.9g Protein; 1.2g Fiber

INGREDIENTS

- 1 teaspoon warm coffee
- 1 teaspoon caramel flavor
- 6 tablespoons butter
- 1 tablespoon peanut butter
- 3 ounces dark chocolate, unsweetened
- 1 teaspoon liquid Monk fruit

DIRECTIONS

1. Microwave the butter and chocolate until they are completely melted.
2. Fold in the remaining Ingredients. Spoon the batter into a foil-lined baking pan, smoothing out the top.
3. Place in your refrigerator for 30 minutes before cutting.
4. Storing
5. Cover your penuche with foil or plastic wrap to prevent drying out; keep in your refrigerator for a week.
6. To freeze, wrap your penuche tightly with foil or place in a heavy-duty freezer bag. Freeze for up to 4 to 6 months. Enjoy!

White Chocolate Fudge Squares

Preparation Time: 15 minutes + chilling time Servings 12

NUTRITION: 202 Calories; 21.3g Fat; 2.3g Carbs; 2.4g Protein; 2.2g Fiber

INGREDIENTS

- 3 ounces white chocolate, unsweetened
- 3/4 cup coconut oil
- 1/3 cup almond milk
- 2 tablespoons Swerve
- 1/8 teaspoon coarse sea salt
- 1 ¼ cups almond butter

DIRECTIONS

1. Microwave the coconut oil, almond butter, and white chocolate until they are melted. Add in the remaining Ingredients and process in your blender.
2. Scrape the mixture into a parchment- lined baking tray. Cut into squares and serve.
3. Storing
4. Cover your fudge squares with foil or plastic wrap to prevent drying out; keep in your refrigerator for a week.

5. To freeze, wrap your fudge squares tightly with foil or place in a heavy-duty freezer bag. Freeze for up to 4 to 6 months. Enjoy!

Coconut and Peanut Bark

Preparation Time: 10 minutes + chilling time Servings 12

NUTRITION: 316 Calories; 31.6g Fat; 4.6g Carbs; 6.6g Protein; 2.6g Fiber

INGREDIENTS

- 3/4 cup coconut oil
- 1/2 teaspoon pure almond extract
- 1/2 cup coconut, shredded
- 3/4 cup peanut butter
- 1 cup powdered Erythritol

DIRECTIONS

1. Melt all Ingredients in a double boiler over medium-low heat.
2. Scrape the batter into a parchment-lined baking pan. Place in your freezer for about 1 hour; break your bark into pieces.
3. Storing
4. Place your bark in airtight containers or Ziploc bags; keep in your refrigerator for 1 month.
5. Place your bark in freezable containers; it will maintain the best quality for 4 months. Defrost in the refrigerator. Bon appétit!

Simple Cauliflower Keto Casserole

Preparation Time: 10minutes Cooking Time: 35 Minutes

Serving: 3

INGREDIENTS

- 1/2- head cauliflower florets
- cup shredded Cheddar cheese
- 1/2- cup heavy cream
- Salt and ground black pepper

DIRECTIONS

1. Preheat the stove to 400 degrees F.
2. Heat a huge pot of gently salted water to the point of boiling and cook cauliflower until delicate yet firm to the nibble, around 10 minutes. Channel.
3. Join cheddar, cream, salt, and pepper in a huge bowl. Mastermind cauliflower in a meal dish and cover with cheddar blend.
4. Heat in the preheated stove until cheddar is bubbly and brilliant darker, around 25 minutes

NUTRITION: Calories 469, Fat 40.9g, Carbs 10g, Sugar 13g, Protein 18.1g

90-Second Keto Bread in a Mug

Preparation Time: 5minutes Cooking Time: 2
Minutes Serving: 4

INGREDIENTS

- 1 tablespoon butter
- 1/3 cup blanched almond flour
- 1 egg
- 1/2 teaspoon baking powder
- 1 pinch salt

DIRECTIONS

1. Spot spread in a microwave-safe mug. Microwave until liquefied, around 15

    seconds Twirl mug until completely covered

2. Consolidate almond flour, egg, heating powder, and salt in the mug; race until smooth.

3. Microwave at most extreme power until set, around 90 seconds

4. Let cool for 2 minutes before cutting.

NUTRITION: Calories 408, Fat 36.4g, Carbs 9.8, Sugar 16g, Protein 14.5g

Keto Cheesecake Cupcakes

Preparation Time: 10minutes Cooking Time:

15 Minutes Serving: 3

INGREDIENTS

- 1/2 cup almond meal
- 1/4 cup butter and 2 eggs
- ounce cream cheese
- 3/4 cup granular no-calorie sucralose sweetener
- 1 teaspoon vanilla extract

DIRECTIONS

1. Preheat stove to 350 degrees F. Line 12 biscuit cups with paper liners.
2. Combine almond supper and margarine in a bowl; spoon into the bottoms of the paper liners and press into a level outside layer.
3. Beat cream cheddar, eggs, sugar, and vanilla concentrate together in a bowl with an electric blender set to medium until smooth; spoon over the outside layer in the paper liners.
4. Prepare in the preheated stove until the cream cheddar blend is about set in the center, 15 to 17 minutes.
5. Give cupcakes a chance to cool at room temperature until cool enough to deal

with. Refrigerate 8 hours to medium-term before serving.

NUTRITION: Calories 204, Fat 20g, Carb 2.1g, Sugar 2.3, Protein 4.9g

CPSIA information can be obtained
at www.ICGtesting.com
Printed in the USA
LVHW080929010621
689026LV00009B/1149